HOW TO PLAY
TENNIS

CLARENCE JONES

TREASURE PRESS

Contents

First published in Great Britain in 1979 by
The Hamlyn Publishing Group Limited

This edition published in 1989 by
Treasure Press
Michelin House
81 Fulham Road
London SW3 6RB

ISBN 1 85051 361 9

Printed in Yugoslavia

Foreword

High among the greatest matches ever played ranks the final of the World Championship of Tennis in May 1972, when Ken Rosewall beat Rod Laver in a tie-breaker fifth set. Too overcome with emotion to do more than mumble, he was unable to convey to the capacity crowd in the Moody Stadium, Dallas, the depth of his happiness and his immense sense of self-fulfilment.

Cynics concentrated their talk on the $50 000 cheque that was part of his prize, and it would be naive to suggest that it was unimportant. But choking back his tears, Rosewall left the president's box and made for the changing room, where he and his friends lived the match over again. The talk continued as they walked to the car park, drove back to the hotel, and sat around the lounge. An hour or so later someone asked to see what was then the biggest cheque ever won at tennis. Rosewall put his hand in a pocket. After fumbling, he went on to search another pocket, and another. No cheque.

A friend volunteered to return to the stadium to see if it was there. The caretaker was found, the stadium was reopened, and the friend hurried to the changing room. There on a chair, completely forgotten, lay Rosewall's $50 000 cheque. . . . So much for the money motive in winning prestigious titles!

This is just one of the many incidents which support my belief that tennis is so great and challenging a game that for the world's best players pleasure in playing ranks equally with the fortunes they earn in prizes. And such fulfilment is not restricted to the stars. Every initiate has his or her personal gold-medal level.

I recall trying to teach an eager but not particularly well co-ordinated eight-year-old the overhead smash. Standing nearby, I tossed a ball into the air and watched him swing . . . and miss the ball completely. Another toss, another miss. Moving a step closer, another toss and another complete miss. So followed a further eighteen or so ever simpler tosses and almost as many complete 'air' shots. More nervous even than when I played in the Davis Cup, I threw yet one more ball . . . and finally he connected. It wasn't a great smash, only adequate in fact, but the smile that spread almost from ear to ear on the little fellow's face was a vivid indication of his immense sense of fulfilment and joy. For me his smile proved a personal highlight for the whole of that season.

One should recognise the importance of any activity which offers such chances of self-expression, fulfilment, aesthetic satisfaction, and sheer pleasure in our highly structured, often restricting, industrial and commercial world. Tennis, with the profound demands it imposes on the technical, tactical, temperamental, physical, and psychological talents of those who play, is an outstanding outlet. It is also a superb route to good health and an excellent way of making new friends.

In this book I have tried to offer learning methods which will help a perceptive reader quickly surmount the difficulties that discourage so many beginners to other games. Follow the instructions and set yourself a target of six separate sessions on a court, preferably within one month. By then you should be maintaining moderate rallies, and, more likely than not, you'll be hooked for the rest of your life.

The book has been written from a right-handed player's viewpoint. Left-handers will have to reverse all directions.   C.J.

Chapter One
Introducing the Game

Standards of Play

Remember the Wimbledon centenary of 1977? Coincidentally, the rules governing international championships had been changed earlier in the year, specifically to allow players under the age of sixteen to compete. The consequence: abundant headlines and stories about Tracy Austin, the fourteen-year-old American girl who reached the third round of the women's singles. The headlines that named her the youngest ever Wimbledon competitor were wrong. Back in 1907, before the lower age limit was introduced, Mita Klimer aged thirteen competed in the women's singles. At the other end of the scale, Jean Borotra contested the Wimbledon mixed doubles at the age of sixty-five . . . and actually won a round. He was still to be seen in action there in centenary year at the age of seventy-eight, though that year he figured in the veterans' event.

Of course, Wimbledon is tennis at its highest levels. On public parks, standards do not reach those breathtaking heights and the age scale extends even further. The youngest child I have ever taught was under four years old: my oldest pupil was seventy-six, though I have a friend aged ninety-three who actually hitchhikes some twenty miles to play. Like my youngest pupil, he enjoys the richest, purest joy from each sweetly hit stroke he makes.

Standards, then, range from absolute beginner to Wimbledon champion. Yet we all possess an inborn, personal gold-medal level. You can

Tennis caters for all ages and all standards, ranging from Wimbledon finals and semi-finals to indoor championships in Rome, to veterans like Stella Risner, aged seventy-six, attacking a visitor on her back-garden

derive pleasure merely by playing. But that pleasure is magnified a hundred times if you strive with all your mind and heart to reach your personal best because this can bring you the deep satisfaction of self-fulfilment.

For those who shy from competition but who still wish to measure their developing skills, there are in Britain and the USA various proficiency awards. In Britain they are promoted by the Professional Coaches Tennis Association, an organisation of around seven hundred men and women who have qualified as members or associate members. To gain the basic and intermediate awards a player must demonstrate the ability to produce a specified range of strokes with a stipulated degree of consistency, score, know a few elementary rules, maintain a ten-stroke rally with the tester, and play a few games with sufficient skill to satisfy the tester that he or she could join a club without ruining everyone else's pleasure. Successful candidates are given certificates and badges. The system is very popular with juniors, and it sets standards which they can normally attain after a few lessons with a qualified coach and a couple of months spent in really conscientious practice.

As well as varying standards of play, there are also different types of player, ranging from fleet-footed retrievers, who scramble back every ball until their frustrated opponents eventually make a mistake, through to aggressors who slam each shot as though they wish to burst the ball. Generally the way a person plays reflects character . . . but not always. The fiercest player I have ever known was a dentist. Why was he fierce? 'I spend all my working days being gentle with patients' teeth,' he explained. 'I have to get rid of all the tension this builds up so I do it playing tennis.'

Clearly, tennis is a game for all reasons . . . and all seasons now that indoor courts are being opened all over the world.

court, to public-park play, to clinics given by stars like Ann Jones and John Lloyd, pictured at Eastbourne, to clubs like Bognor L.T.C., where card games while away the time spent waiting for courts.

9

Rules of the Game

Tennis is a game played on a court either by two people, one each side of a net which divides the court into two equal parts, or by four people, two each side of the net. At competition level it is normally played man against man or woman against woman (singles), or by four men or women (doubles), or one man and one woman each side of the net (mixed doubles).

The net is 3 feet (0·91 m) high in the middle and 6 inches (15·24 cm) higher at the support posts, which are positioned 3 feet outside the outer sideline. Diagram 1 shows the dimensions of the court and other relevant details.

The object of each point is to hit the ball in such a way that either (a) it bounces twice within the opponent's half of the court before it can be returned, or (b) it cannot in fact be returned to the other half of the court. The opponents continue hitting the ball to and fro until one or the other places a shot that cannot be reached or returned successfully.

Each point begins with a service. The server stands with both feet behind the baseline anywhere between the centre mark and the sideline of the singles or doubles court, depending upon the number of play-ers. He or she throws a ball into the air and strikes it before it reaches the ground, the aim being to place it in the opponent's service court diagonally opposite. If the first try is faulty – the ball being misplaced or missed entirely – a second attempt is allowed. The service is declared a 'let' if the ball touches the strap or band at the top of the net before falling into the correct service court, in which case that service does not count and the server must serve again. The receiver must allow the served ball to bounce; all subsequent shots in the rally may either be vol-leyed (the ball being struck before it bounces) or hit as groundstrokes (the ball being struck after it bounces). The server makes the first service from the right-hand side, moves to the left side for the second point, and then alternates sides for the subse-quent points.

One player continues serving until a game is completed. The opponent then serves for one game, when ser-vice reverts to the first player. In doubles, however, it becomes the turn of the original server's partner to serve for a game and the original receiver's partner completes the cycle.

The first player to win four points wins the game unless the score reaches three points all. When this

Diagram 1: The dimensions of a tennis court. If you want to be a winner, you should study 'court geometry' until you can talk it in your sleep. Do you know, for instance, that the distance from the junction of your singles sideline and baseline to your opponent's centre mark measures 79 ft 1½ inches (24·12 m)?

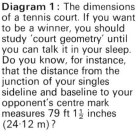

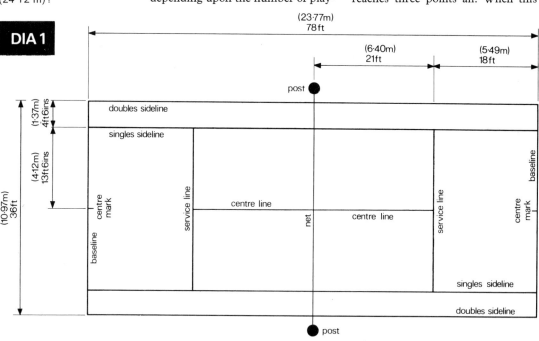

occurs, the game continues until one of the players or pairs establishes a lead of two points. Tennis scoring traditionally does not use 1, 2, 3 etc., but 15, 30, 40, and for zero the word used is 'love'. If both opponents win three points, the word 'deuce' is employed. The next point is called 'advantage server' or 'advantage receiver', according to who wins it. If the same player wins the following point, that player has, of course, won the game. If he or she loses it, the score reverts to deuce and so on until one player establishes that two-point lead.

Tennis matches are usually won by the first player to win two sets; such matches are called 'best of three sets'. At Wimbledon the men's events are 'best of five sets', the first player or pair to win three sets being the winner.

The first player to reach six games wins the set except when the score is 5-5, or 'five games all'. Traditionally, the set then continued until one player established a two-game lead, e.g. 8-6, 14-12, 31-29. Today these 'advantage sets' have largely been

Left: The ball must touch the line to be in. This is a rule which is frequently misunderstood. The further ball touches the line so it is 'in'; the nearer ball overhangs the line, but is not actually touching it, so it is 'out'.

Above left: The start of a service. So long as neither foot touches the playing area, including the baseline, or crosses and touches the ground on the opposite side of the centre mark, *before* the ball leaves the racket, the service will be OK. The server can even jump forward and hover in mid-air in front of the line so long as the ball is hit before either foot grounds.

Above right: Here the server has already hit the ball so no footfault, although his right foot is inside the court.

11

Above: No footfault here so long as Borg's feet hover *above* the court. Once either foot touches any area other than that behind the baseline between the centre mark and the sideline, it is a different story.

ousted by the 'tie-break', which usually comes into operation when the score in games reaches 6-6, or 8-8 at Wimbledon.

In the tie-break, a final deciding game is played. This game, and with it the set, goes to the first player to win seven points, again unless the score reaches six points all. Then the tie-break continues until one player establishes a two-point lead, e.g. 9-7 or 16-14. Some countries use a 'first to score five points' tie-break. One such is the USA, where they also permit what they call 'No Ad scoring'. This uses the straightforward nu-

12

Above: Three examples of foot faulting: standing on the line at the moment of impact (*left*), one foot grounded inside the court as the ball is hit (*centre*), and one foot on the wrong side of the centre mark while hitting the ball (*right*).

Far left: The ball must pass the net before it is volleyed. This volley is OK: the ball had crossed the net before the player hit it.

Left: Here the player volleyed the ball before it crossed the net so he loses the point. If the ball had bounced his side of the net and then spun back over it, he could have leaned over the net to hit the ball, provided he did not touch the net with his racket, body, or clothing.

merical terminology of 1, 2, 3, 4 instead of the 15, 30, 40, game; the first to score 4 wins the game.

It is customary in tournament matches for players or pairs to change ends at regular intervals, namely after the first, third, fifth, and every subsequent alternate game. Each set is a separate entity so if one set finishes at 6-3, say, there is an immediate change of ends and then another after the first game of the following set. In the case of a tie-break the players change ends after every six points, the whole tie-break counting as one game.

13

Chapter Two
Equipment

The Modern Racket

Tennis had its origins in simple games of handball, but power was naturally limited to what the human hand could tolerate until someone tried using a wooden bat. By the mid 1550s this development had led to the introduction of frames strung with gut or gut substitutes. These early rackets have evolved into the gleaming, streamlined equipment of today. Currently a significant percentage of rackets are made from materials other than wood, though wooden rackets still maintain a substantial majority. Originally they were made from single strips of suitable wood, the piece being softened, bent, and fixed around a former and then left to assume its shape and harden. Not until the late 1780s did it become customary to fashion the handle separately and bind head and handle together.

The manufacture of a wooden racket. Six stages in the making of a Dunlop Maxply Fort (*reading across*): 1. thin strips of wood or laminations are peeled from steam-softened logs; 2. continuous laminations covered with adhesive are laid round a mould wide enough for three rackets; 3. once the mahogany throat-piece and leatheroid inserts have been positioned, the frame is pressed into shape with several tons of pressure; 4. parallel rotating saws separate the bends into three rackets; 5. thirty-two automatic drills prepare the holes which will take the stringing (the last two drills nearest the handle are used separately later); 6. after painting, the trimmings are added and then comes the final lacquering.

Metal was first used in the 1880s but the finished product proved heavy and clumsy. Lightweight steel rackets came off a Birmingham, England, production line in the 1920s and these bear a remarkable resemblance to many made today, though the modern taste for 'cosmetic design' has produced shapes and colours which mask the basic similarity.

The 1970s heralded the introduction of scientifically conceived alternatives to the steel and aluminium which were growing in popularity. Today one can choose from multi-laminated wood, steel, aluminium, glass fibre, boron, graphite, and many blendings of these and other materials. With any racket carrying the name of an internationally famous maker one may be assured that production has been carefully monitored and strict quality-control exercised.

In the manufacture of rackets the

constant need for compromise presents many practical problems. Wood absorbs shock vibrations more certainly than steel or aluminium but, ounce for ounce, is less strong. Makers who believe in flexibility tend to concentrate on wood, using thin strips of many varieties, such as ash, hickory, or willow, to build up laminated frames. In the 1970s it has become fashionable to incorporate one or more non-wooden laminations or to strengthen the head with overlays of glass fibre or graphite, the most promising of all the new materials. Graphite frames can be fabricated so that lateral or longitudinal flexibility is inbuilt where needed and to any required degree. Once the trade of artisans, racket manufacture today is an exact science working to extremely precise specifications.

Choosing Your Racket

Your racket is the 'tool' with which you perform so it makes sense to select a model which seems as nearly as possible an extension of your arm and hand when in use. By all means choose one which appeals to your eye but do not allow superficialities to sway your judgement. Study design basics and make sure your racket matches your requirements.

It must feel comfortable in dynamic situations; that means when you are actually playing, not simply when you make stylish, imaginary strokes in front of your bedroom mirror. I am not trying to minimise the value of developing easy, flowing strokes by rehearsing them without a ball, but a racket tends to feel heavier when a ball weighing around 2 ounces (57 g) is pounding against it every 2 seconds or so. Grip size, too, usually feels a little larger in action.

It is impossible to generalise about weight or grip size. But ignore that oft repeated myth 'the heavier the racket the greater the power'. It can be shown mathematically that doubling the speed of the racket-head without increasing its mass is almost six times as speed effective as doubling the racket-head mass and keeping its speed at impact constant. As a guide, most of today's top male stars use a 13½-ounce (382·71 g) racket

with a 4⅝-inch (0·12 m) grip. Top woman player Chris Evert is a powerful hitter, and her racket breakdown is as follows: frame 12¾ ounces (350·8 g), gut ⅜ ounce (10·62 g), grip ¼ ounce (7·08 g), the total 13 ounces (368·54 g) or marginally less.

Next, frame flexibility. The myths proliferate here too. But it is possible to state quite categorically that the more rigid the 'hitting platform' (or racket head), the greater the power. Once flexibility enters the equation, a factor called the co-efficient of restitution assumes importance. Without delving into mechanical engineering, this means that the rebound time of even the most whippy racket is longer than the time the ball is on

Rackets come and go in sufficient shapes and sizes to satisfy almost any idiosyncracy. Yet they have not changed radically in well over fifty years. Can you guess which racket is more than fifty years old? The answer appears at the bottom of the following page.

the strings. Therefore the backward give of the frame 'rides' the impact, reducing the shock and producing better control and a pleasanter feel than a rigid frame. However, if you are a strong, vigorous person who loves power, choose one of the more rigid rackets, one made from graphite or reinforced glass fibre perhaps.

If it has been carefully designed, the high-frequency, elbow-damaging shock vibrations set up by mis-hitting will have been reduced by damping techniques, but some lower frequency vibrations must be transmitted to the brain via the hand if a player is to experience 'touch'. Damping one without the other presents complex problems. The search for ways of reducing shock without undue loss of overall power has led to some novel ways of stringing . . . and to the jumbo-sized rackets which are growing in popularity. These are specially valuable to senior players – say those over forty who sadly and inevitably hit more and more off-centre shots. Jumbo rackets have larger 'sweet spots', so the number of shocks is reduced . . . and also the incidence of tennis elbow.

Stringing presents another dilemma. Natural gut possesses the inherent elasticity of young animal tissue but it is considerably less durable than the synthetic strings now available. Unfortunately, synthetics are far less elastic, and they sop up energy when ball meets strings; in plain terms, they reduce power and touch. Nonetheless, for beginners and intermediate players durability is probably more important than feel.

Another popular myth is 'the tighter the stringing, the greater the power'. But there is, in fact, an optimum tension for every frame and set of strings, bound up yet again with the relative co-efficients of restitution of ball and strings. In the case of a Dunlop Maxply Fort and an officially authorised ball, this optimum tension is around 48 pounds (21·8 kg). See Table 1 opposite. These tensions are for fast surfaces; on slow courts they can be reduced by a couple of pounds (0·9 kg). Clean hitters of the ball might increase

them by 2 or 3 pounds (0·9 or 1·3 kg).

When buying a racket, follow these rules.
1 Choose an internationally famed maker and model.
2 If in doubt, persuade a coach or knowledgeable friend to help you.
3 Buy from a reputable store, sports shop, or qualified professional.
4 Swing many rackets vigorously before making your final choice, noting how well you can control the racket head.
5 Think in terms of $13\frac{1}{2}$ ounces (382·71 g) in weight, even balance, and a $4\frac{5}{8}$-inch (0·12 m) grip for men, and of 13 ounces (368·54 g), even balance, and an approximately $4\frac{1}{2}$-inch (0·11 m) grip for women.
6 For pleasure and performance, choose top-quality natural gut, bearing in mind that it is expensive, but for economy and hard wear be satisfied with man-made strings, preferably going for Staytite, Super Eternyl, or Hy-O-Sheep.

Courts and Balls

Until July 1977 the game's official title was 'Lawn Tennis', no matter the surface on which it was played. During that month the International Lawn Tennis Federation, the world ruling body, dropped that word 'lawn' from its title and also from the name of the game, formal recognition that grass courts are slowly disappearing and that far and away the greater number of major championships, tournaments, and representative matches are now staged on an immense variety of other surfaces.

Enthusiasts had first begun looking for alternative surfaces when they realised that play on grass was possible only from May to September. Macadam roads seemed tough and smooth so courts were made with that material; one hundred years later they still are the solution when cost surpasses all other considerations. However, such courts are hard on the feet and on tennis balls so they have never been greatly liked.

The pioneers continued their

Answer to question on page 15
The top-left racket was made over fifty years ago.

search for alternatives. Concrete was smoother and, though hard on the feet, it produced a fast and satisfying game. Such courts still abound in California but Britain's variable climate created problems which, to this day, have never been completely solved. The technique used in TennisQuick produced perhaps the best all-weather concrete courts until the development of plastics in the 1960s.

Closely packed brickdust on a carefully constructed foundation and a well-drained sub-surface is, when skilfully maintained, still the most pleasant of all the winter surfaces. What happens if lack of time and money limit maintenance is evident when one examines the loose-surface red courts scattered around the world.

Indoors, artificial grass carpets are sometimes used, though not so widely as the rubber and simulated rubber courts favoured by the promoters of the big-money international tournaments. Wood is probably the best of all indoor surfaces because it normally provides a fast and, most important, satisfying game for the not-quite-so-good enthusiast.

Plastic sprayed over a slightly cushioned lamination is a feature of the latest generation of artificial surfaces. The material can be varied to provide playing speeds adjusted to the specific demands of purchasers. Such courts are extremely costly but wonderfully satisfying on which to play. Travel the world and you will find dozens of innovative courts:

crushed sea shells, pounded down ant-hills, compressed cow dung, and linoleum are but four that come to my mind.

The speed of a court depends primarily on the resistance to the ball offered by the top surface but this can be varied significantly by the hardness of the sub-surface. Polished wood provides the fastest game, followed by closely cut grass on a firm surface. Coarse asphalt is about the slowest. Experience enables one to estimate the speed of a court by looking at its surface and testing its hardness.

Originally, tennis was played with uncovered rubber balls. These were smooth and difficult to control. Woollen covers provided the air drag needed for control and covered balls took over in the 1880s. The softness and responsiveness of wool maximised control and speed. During the 1920s the hand stitching of these covers was replaced by gluey solutions and stitchless balls are with us still. Unfortunately wool is costly and less hard-wearing than nylon and other plastics so covers today are made from blends of natural and synthetic materials.

Stages in the manufacture of a Dunlop Fort tennis ball: 1. the rubber core of each ball is fitted with two covers of melton cloth dipped in a rubber solution, the first being attached by machine, the second by hand; 2. after the final inspection, the rebound factor is tested by making sure that under a given weight the ball will deflect by a specified amount.

Table 1

Class of player	Natural gut	Synthetic strings
novice	46 lb/20·9 kg	44 lb/19·9 kg
average	48 lb/21·8 kg	45 lb/20·4 kg
county or good club	50 lb/22·7 kg	47 lb/21·3 kg
good tournament	53 lb/24 kg	50 lb/22·7 kg

The ball has to conform to specified sizes and weights, and fall within stipulated degrees of compression. The latter is usually achieved by inserting a small pellet during manufacture which turns into gas after the ball has been sealed. The stipulated lower limit is no greater than the pressure of the earth's atmosphere and nowadays many makers produce 'pressureless' balls. These have a limitless shelf-like but they feel deader to the touch than gas-filled balls which are not too old and deflated.

Dress and Shoes

Why bother about your clothes and shoes? That seems to be the attitude of many people I see playing in public parks.

On a purely practical note, competitive success in tennis depends on confidence, and confidence is the child of competence. Clean, absorbent, well-fitting clothes which in no way restrict the rapid movements and joint-testing contortions of tennis make significant contributions to that competence. Then again, most people feel mentally and physically uplifted when spruced up for a special occasion and it is my opinion that, if you truly wish to improve, each time you step onto a tennis court should be a special occasion. Surely, too, if you enjoy playing any kind of game and if you gain fulfilment through improvement, you should take a pride in your appearance when playing.

Historically, all-white clothes, both for men and women, have predominated on the courts though coloured sweaters have always been acceptable. Between the two World Wars it was customary for women's doubles pairs to wear matching cardigans, head-bands, and, quite often, dresses, socks, and shoes. This unofficial practice was codified on the World Championship of Tennis circuit in the 1970s when fines – of $500 or even more – were imposed on players

Let comfort guide your choice when selecting kit. Clothes with a high percentage of cotton or wool are best because they absorb perspiration. Stan Smith, Bjorn Borg, and Chris Evert have all gone for easy-to-wear clothes which look good, always an important psychological consideration.

who failed to wear matching outfits.

Nowadays coloured outfits are the rule rather than the exception and the choice offered by any enterprising store or specialist sports shop should satisfy the average enthusiast. I would make only the following points. Movement produces heat which dissipates in sweat. Left on the body, sweat causes trouble so wear absorbent clothes next to the skin. Prevent chills by immediately donning a sweater, preferably wool, the moment you finish your game or match . . . or if the pace slows down and you begin to feel cold. Try to take at least one change of clothes with you, and wash your outfit after each day's play.

Feet take a tremendous pounding so select well-fitting, adequately ventilated shoes. Examine the soles to judge if they will yield the traction you prefer: some players like to slide, others to have a firmer foothold. Sole thickness is a matter of personal taste. Generalising, I suggest thicker rather than thinner, softer rather than harder. And in this context take care over the selection of your socks. Like ill-fitting shoes, tight socks restrict the feet and can lead to corns and bunions. They should be absorbent, soft, and washed carefully after every use.

19

Chapter Three
Grips

The 'eastern' forehand grip. To obtain the grip used by 90 per cent of top-class professionals, grasp the racket in your left hand and place the palm of your right hand flat against the racket strings. These should be perpendicular to the ground. Bring your right hand back to the end of the handle. Shake hands with it and you have the eastern forehand. Note that the 'V' formed by your thumb and first finger is slightly behind the racket, forehand strokes always being made in the direction of the arrow in picture 3. For additional clarity, the 'V' has been marked to show how the position of the hand changes for the different grips.

Your racket is the implement with which you control the ball. The way you hold it in your hand – your grip – determines your swing. There are several grips designed to yield you maximum effectiveness in various situations. However, slight variations may not cause much loss of effectiveness, and the greater comfort derived from a swing which you find natural may more than compensate for any theoretical loss.

The way you grip your racket also governs your touch, that is how strongly the feel of ball on racket strings is transmitted by your neural system to your brain. In developing your strokes, experiment with tiny variations of finger and hand position until you discover those which yield the best touch and surest control.

Watch a few matches between top-class players and you will see that the majority of shots are hit when the ball is approximately 30 inches (0·76 m) above ground level. More than 90 per cent of tournament players find that the so-called 'eastern grips', forehand and backhand, are best suited to hitting balls that bounce around that height. If you learn on damp courts, where the ball continually skids through low, you may find the 'chopper grip' particularly suitable. This is the most flexible grip of all, but you need a very strong wrist and grip to use it effectively. If you play on courts where the bounce is high with balls that have lost their cover nap, your best grip may be the 'western', though your increased power will have to be set against a reduction in reach and flow. Once you have found these grips, practise swinging your racket for a minute or two whenever you have a chance so that you and your racket eventually feel as one.

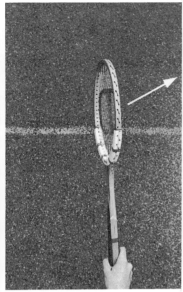  

To obtain the standard 'eastern' backhand grip, loosen your forehand grip and swivel your hand so that the 'V' is now slightly behind the handle if the ball is being hit in the direction of the arrow. Note that the thumb is slightly across the back of the handle so bracing the racket a little when hitting the ball.

The chopper grip. With the 'V' on top of the handle this grip is standard for powerful servers. Some strong-wristed people use it for all shots and are known as 'one-grip players'. Using it for serving necessitates a twist of the wrist at impact (see page 26).

The 'western' grip. Beginners, specially on courts where the ball regularly bounces to shoulder height, often hold their rackets with the 'V' far behind the handle. But this grip is totally unsuited to courts where the bounce is consistently low.

 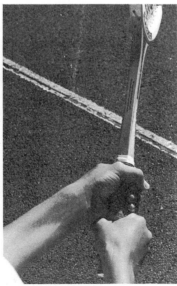 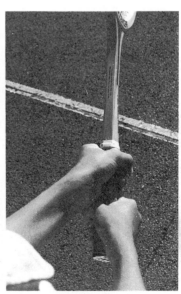

Grips used by exponents of the double-handed backhand vary enormously, principally in accordance with the predominant hand. If the player is right-hand orientated, the 'V' will probably be somewhat behind

the handle and the left palm will also be behind it for bracing and extra thrust. However, if the arms play an equal role, both 'V's may be on top of the handle. With left-arm dominance, *that* hand is likely to take up an

eastern forehand grip, whereas the right hand may well be used to help pull the racket through the stroke.

Here are three of the many slight variations that are adopted.

Chapter Four
Service

There is one stroke in tennis which is entirely dependent on you. Nothing the opponent does can affect that stroke. It starts every point played, and it is, of course, the service.

The overarm service was introduced at Wimbledon in 1878 by A. T. Myers. It did not help him much, but the generations who followed developed it into the most important stroke in the game, hence the 'ace', a service which speeds the ball past the receiver without that player being able even to touch it with his or her racket. In the 1932 Wimbledon men's final Ellsworth Vines served 17 aces in 12 games against Bunny Austin. In 1976 John Feaver served 42 aces in 28 games against John Newcombe. Every ace is the equivalent of raising one's overall game a couple of classes so time spent developing a world-class service is never wasted.

The Throwing Action

Anyone who can throw a ball strongly can develop such a service. That action is not achieved by flexible arm muscles alone. It also depends on co-ordinating leg, hip, and shoulder movements. All must pivot in unison with the swing of the arm so that at the moment of release their individual speeds are cumulative and combine with the actual speed of the arm movement. So it is with the service. Because the muscles around the hip area are the heaviest in the entire body, correct timing of the moment they enter the action is tremendously important. That moment should be fractionally before the forward swing of the arm. Other vital factors are firstly the way the shoulders are stretched wide so that the throw of the racket at the ball is as long as possible, and secondly the way the left arm is pushed high into the air so that the ball is *placed* in the position for hitting rather than thrown.

In the USA, where baseball is even more of a summer fetish than cricket in England, many youngsters from three or four years of age upwards imagine themselves nationally famous pitchers. They, their brothers, sisters, and most kids in the country spend hours each week throwing balls at one another, 'grooving' their muscles and developing their elasticity and explosive powers in the way needed not only for pitching a base-

Top-class serving is based on a powerful throwing action. This necessitates stretching the throwing arm and shoulder as far back as possible and raising the upper arm until it is at least parallel with the ground before bending the forearm. (The other arm and shoulder should meanwhile be stretched forwards.) The forearm, after dropping backwards and downwards while keeping well away from the body, should then be thrust vigorously upwards. Note how the right side of the body pivots to add force to the throw, and how the right leg is pushed into the upward thrust by the foot. The throwing arm should travel upwards and outwards after releasing the ball to ensure that the follow-through is unchecked and vigorous.

ball but also for serving at tennis. Maybe this is one of the reasons why the States produces so many excellent tennis players.

Compare the picture sequences in this section showing a player throwing and serving the ball. The action is identical. Study the player's fore and upper arm at the moment he bends his elbow before the final, explosive section of the throw. Notice how between that moment, when the upper arm is parallel with the ground, and the moment he releases the ball, his right side pivots through an angle of 90 degrees to face the net.

If you do not already throw this way, practise until you can. Go on practising until you can throw a tennis ball approximately 70 yards (64 m) if you are a man, 50 yards (45·7 m) if you are a woman. To save

measuring, stand at the back netting of a tennis court and throw a ball clean over the netting at the other end of the court. To relate throwing a ball to throwing the racket head at a ball, find an old unused tennis racket and practise throwing that. You may become unpopular if you throw it over the net and onto the court so turn round and throw it clear of the baseline into the back netting, using the chopper grip shown on page 21.

The service 'throwing action' should flow smoothly and harmoniously, beginning slowly and building up to maximum speed in the 'crunch area' – the 12 inches (0·30 m) before and the 12 inches after the hit (Americans call this the 'zip area') – and then coming to a smooth conclusion. Imagine a giant jet aircraft speeding up for take off and still

Diagram 2: How the wrist is used to project a cannon-ball service without spin. Note not only the outward turn at the second stage, with the racket face 'looking' along the line on which the ball is travelling, but also how it stays on that line after the hit. The wrist flick adds speed to the racket head at impact and so makes the service faster.

Bjorn Borg owes much of his amazing success to his formidable service, as pictured in this sequence. Note the wide stretch of his shoulders, the use of his left arm to place the ball in position and the way he maintains a flowing action by keeping his racket clear of his back. See the power he develops through the body pivot, the extra speed he obtains by using his wrist, the vigour of his follow-through, and the careful way his eyes stay focused on the ball.

—— theoretical path of service hit by player over 6ft 2ins tall

――― theoretical path of service hit by player of average height

----- actual path of sliced service hit by player of average height

baseline   service line   net   service line   baseline

Diagram 3: In practice, gravity prevents a ball from travelling in a straight line. Instead it curves downward, a tendency which can be increased by the use of spin. This virtually eliminates any major advantage in being tall.

Above: This strobe sequence shows the path of the racket head during a world-class player's service. The swing is good but the even spacing between each stop reveals a lack of zip-area acceleration.

Above right: Use of the chopper grip develops maximum power in service. It also necessitates a wrist turn to ensure that the ball travels straight. Here two players hit the netting to learn this wrist turn. Compare the wrist position in this exercise with that in the second stage of Diagram 2 on page 23 to understand the movement.

speeding after touch down until it is safely 'on course' on the runway. The movement should flow continuously, but it may help to think of the continuity in two phases: first placing the ball and racket in juxtaposition for the hit and then the hit itself.

Co-ordination doesn't stop there. Grip is important too. Top-class servers use the chopper grip and this involves an outward turn of the wrist when actually hitting the ball. Diagram 2 shows this vital wrist action in a flat, or no spin, service. You can learn the technique with a simple exercise which involves hitting the stop netting as shown above right. The other important point in co-ordination is the ability to place the ball in the correct position so that the swiftly moving 'throw' of the racket face hits the ball over the net and

into the correct service area. Note the choice of that word 'place', rather than 'throw', when speaking of the ball.

A further tip: it may help your timing if you start the service by getting the racket moving and then place the ball in position. Finally, a 'must' if you wish to develop and maintain a strong service.. Avoid trying to 'muscle' the ball with brute force. Let the racket do the work with a firm, smooth, accelerating swing.

Slice and Kick Services

You have to be more than 6 feet 2 inches (1·88 m) tall to serve a ball which will descend in a straight line from your upstretched racket to fall within your opponent's service court. See Diagram 3. In practice, gravity

26

has some effect, curving the ball's flight downwards by approximately 9 inches (0·23 m) in a tournament-standard, fast delivery. But this still does not give much of a safety margin when you try to produce an ace by slamming over a no-spin cannonball.

The solution is to apply a little slice: Diagram 4 shows you how. Slice is the name given to a spin obtained by hitting the ball to the right and slightly below its centre spot; see point x in Diagram 5 on page 28. It causes the ball both to dip slightly in flight when it is served and to curve from right to left as it speeds towards the opponent. It also tends to keep the ball low after the service bounce.

How much dip and curve there are depend on the ratio of slice to speed. Lots of slice and not too much speed

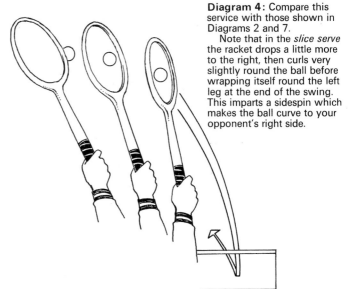

Diagram 4: Compare this service with those shown in Diagrams 2 and 7.

Note that in the *slice serve* the racket drops a little more to the right, then curls very slightly round the ball before wrapping itself round the left leg at the end of the swing. This imparts a sidespin which makes the ball curve to your opponent's right side.

Diagram 5: To slice or twist a service, the ball is struck off centre to impart spin. For the twist the ball is struck upwards at *y*, for the slice sideways at *x*. The actual spin is variable but it approximates to the direction shown by the arrows if the ball is travelling away from you.

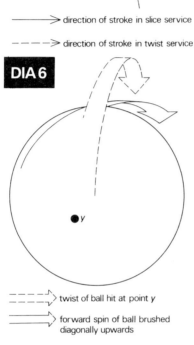

DIA 5

$\longrightarrow$ direction of stroke in slice service

$----\rightarrow$ direction of stroke in twist service

Diagram 6: The direction and angle of twist imparted to a ball is a direct result of the combined forward and sideways path of the racket while it is in contact with the ball.

DIA 6

$----\rightarrow$ twist of ball hit at point *y*

$\longrightarrow$ forward spin of ball brushed diagonally upwards

will accentuate dip and curve. Less slice and more speed will reduce both. How low the ball stays after it has bounced is also affected by the surface of the court. A smooth surface offers little resistance so the ball skids. That is why service dominates most matches played on the ultra-smooth, short grass courts at Wimbledon. Rougher surfaces bite at the ball, giving it a greater upward kick.

You can take advantage of this kick by applying an upward, twisting spin. Do it by hitting the ball to the left and slightly below the centre spot (again see Diagram 5, point *y*) and by brushing the racket strings diagonally across the back of the ball in the direction of the arrow in that diagram. This 'brushing' action spins the ball clockwise, whereas the forward impulse of the swing spins it vertically. The resultant spin in flight is a mixture of the two actions (see Diagram 6).

If the server gets well under the ball and brushes it strongly, it will curve from left to right as it travels to the opponent's service court and, on bouncing, it will kick and break in the same direction. Diagram 7 illustrates that serving action. The stronger the forward impulse of the spin, the smaller will be the curve and the break. This type of service is called the 'American twist'. Because of its trajectory and kick, it can be an effective form of attack against a

To gain accuracy, racket and ball control, and to learn the use of the wrist, practise bouncing a ball with the edge of the frame. Next practise bouncing a ball with a downwards, brushing movement of the strings on the upper side of the ball. This gives you the feel of imparting spin. When you can do this a few times, end the exercise by suddenly turning the wrist and bouncing the ball straight up in the air for 20 to 40 feet (6·12 to 12·21 m). This develops the powerful wrist action needed for fast serving.

DIA 7

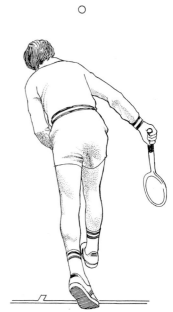

Diagram 7: Compare this service with those shown in Diagrams 2 and 4.

In the *kick or twist serve* the racket drops further to the left and there is a pronounced back bend. Both factors allow the racket to sweep up and across the ball from left to right. The bite of the spin depends on how strongly you can straighten your back and flick your wrist to make the racket snap

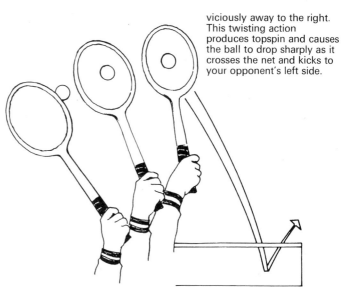

right-handed player's backhand.

In contrast, the slice serve is useful against players who find difficulty in coping with low returns that curve away to their right (the server's left). Indeed, such services played an important part in Arthur Ashe's surprise upset of the supposedly invincible Jimmy Connors in the 1975 Wimbledon men's singles final.

Spin, be it slice or American twist, is both a sound method of increasing ball control and a way of harrassing the player receiving service. The harrassment can be intensified through subtle variations of speed and degrees of spin.

In serving, as in all shot making, always remember that automatic, unthinking repetition frees the receiver from fear of the unexpected.

viciously away to the right. This twisting action produces topspin and causes the ball to drop sharply as it crosses the net and kicks to your opponent's left side.

The quickest way to give a beginner a sound technique for groundstrokes. In an alert position, minus racket, he moves towards the line of the oncoming ball, hand out in readiness, and lets it fall into his hand. Once he shows proficiency, he can repeat the routine with a racket. Next he is encouraged to give a little tap at impact. Then to increase power without using a significant back swing.

Chapter Five

Groundstrokes

The Fundamentals

There is much to be said for 'doing what comes naturally', but in tennis the strokes of good-class players seldom conform completely to this precept. Contrast such players with the enthusiast who lacks the discernment to rectify his or her misconceptions, and who progresses only slowly, if at all. What a sad waste of energy. The fundamentals are after all so easy to understand.

Good stroke-making depends upon five basic factors:

1 the correct gauging of the speed of the approaching ball;
2 the speed of your racket head when you hit the ball;
3 the firmness of your grip, wrist, and arm at the moment of impact;
4 the length of time your racket and the ball are in contact; and
5 the angle at which the strings are travelling during contact time.

But the most vital part of any stroke is that period when your racket head is traversing the zip area, the 12 inches (0·30 m) immediately before and after the hit. The preparation and follow-through of the stroke are important only insofar as they lead up to and then ensure complete racket-head control in the zip area. Until you can control the zip-area action, you cannot control the ball, and without ball control you cannot become an accurate, powerful hitter.

The routine shown on this page is the quickest way for a beginner to acquire basic strokes which can develop into adequacy for top-class competition. It concentrates on the zip area and adds the trimmings of back swing and follow-through by natural development. The system was invented by Canadian coach Peter Burwash, and in using it he has had beginners maintaining fifty-stroke rallies within 10 minutes of picking up a racket for the first time. Though designed primarily for be-

ginners, the racket routine is a valuable discipline for the 'slashers' who proliferate in public parks. This is because the essence of controlled, powerful strokes is a slow swing with extra thrust of the racket (and the shoulder) at the start of the zip area.

Most beginners when trying to hit hard simply slash at the ball. In other words they take their rackets too far back before hurling them forwards at the ball as fast as possible. All that happens is that they lose control and the racket is in fact decelerating by the time it hits the ball.

The rhythm of a sound and forceful stroke is slow to fast with a conscious attempt to thrust the racket head through the ball at the start of the zip area. Control the speed of your arm-swing accordingly and develop the extra power you seek by pivoting your hips and shoulders in unison with your arm. This can increase considerably the racket-head speed at the moment of impact, enable you to maintain a firm grip on the handle, and add 50 per cent to the speed of the shot.

Footwork

Quick, certain footwork is a vital ingredient of all strokes, especially those made after the ball has bounced. In waiting between shots, you should be evenly and lightly balanced on the balls of the feet, knees a little bent and weight slightly forward.

Avoid over-crouching because in straightening up you have to raise the body against the pull of gravity and that slows down movement. The first step should be made the moment the ball's direction has been read. If it is coming to the forehand of a right-hander, the first movement should normally be with the right foot and leg; if to the backhand, with the left foot. That first movement should be tiny, perhaps 6 inches (0·15 m) in all and certainly not more than a foot (0·30 m), unless you have to dash at top speed to chase down a fast shot

which seems miles out of reach. It is this step which sets the pace and rhythm of the entire run to the ball. It should be so judged that you arrive at the hitting position with the right foot forward for a forehand, the left foot for a backhand.

Time and distance must be so keenly assessed that on the forehand the left leg and foot can move forward in unison with the swing of the racket, the full weight being transferred onto the left, front leg at the exact moment the racket hits the ball. On the backhand the full weight should go forward onto the right leg at the moment of impact.

The interim run between that first, temporising, rhythm-setting step and the final stride forward in time with the racket swing should normally consist of small, light, smooth steps so that the whole body flows towards the ball. A jerky run usually means a jerky stroke; a smooth run increases the chances of a flowing, powerful, well-timed stroke.

Now comes the crunch. Neither this book nor any coach can *make* you do anything. They can tell and show you how in all its details but then it is up to you to LEARN what you need. You have to unearth a kindred spirit and go on court together. There the two of you should gently hit balls to and fro while concentrating meticulously on the key advice given on these pages.

The correct footwork from a position of readiness to hit either a backhand or forehand drive. Note how the player turns sideways, pointing the front shoulder at the ball, takes the racket back, and

then steps forward into the correct position in time with the swing. Full weight goes onto the front leg at the moment of impact. (Both sequences run from centre picture upwards.)

The forehand drive. Note the position of readiness: racket head forward, knees bent, eyes concentrating on the ball to pick up direction immediately. Then the right foot turns, a small step forward with the left leg, and the racket moves back in early preparation. In picture 3 the racket is still continuing its back swing while the player moves to the correct position. In picture 4 the racket is fully back as the player steps towards the ball, his left arm pointing to help sighting and balance.

Racket, shoulder, and hips pivot as one to hit the ball powerfully, and the player begins a forward run to the net. Then, as the racket wraps round the left shoulder, the right shoulder and hip end their strong, power-giving pivot and the forward run continues with the head still down. There has been no trace of jerking in the entire stroke in spite of the run forward. Note how head and shoulders still form a line with the body.

The Forehand

Modern tennis courts tend to be significantly slower than those which were made in the years between the World Wars. This increases the need for at least one especially powerful stroke in addition to a strong service. In most cases, players concentrate on the forehand drive made after the ball has bounced.

Forehand drives are made on the right-hand side of right-handed players, and they are so named because the front part of the lower arm and wrist are facing the ball at the moment it is struck. Power is mainly dependent on the speed of the racket head at the moment it hits the ball. The weight of the racket head is also significant but this is not a constant factor since effective weight – or mass – varies with the strength and solidity of the player's grip.

The most solid grip consistent with flexibility of movement is the eastern, shown on page 20. Used by at least 90 per cent of the world's best players, it should be adopted by all beginners and novices except in those rare cases when the player possesses an outstanding aptitude when holding the racket in some other way.

It is often said that the racket should feel like part of the hand, and certainly there is a great similarity between hitting a ball with the palm of the hand and with a racket, as the pictures opposite illustrate. Yet I believe it is better to handle and swing the racket at all possible moments until it feels like part of the *arm*, a natural lever which extends from the shoulder to the tip of the racket frame.

Remembering that power is a product of racket-head speed and grip strength, strive constantly to develop a sense of timing and a swing that starts the racket flowing forward with a slow but constant acceleration that reaches top speed at the moment of impact. Simultaneously, ensure that your grip is strongest during the moments before, during, and after the actual hit.

There is a limit to the speed at which your arm can swing the racket and still retain maximum grip strength. Extra racket-head speed – and power – should be developed through body pivot. When the ball is correctly struck, there is a wonderfully sweet feeling of hand, arm, shoulder, hips, and legs all working

To develop the conception of your racket feeling like a part of your arm, hit a few balls over the net with the palm of your hand.

in unison and punching solidly right behind the ball as it speeds towards the target at which you decided to aim your shot.

Have confidence in your stroke. Concentrate on hitting the ball at or just after the top of its bounce. Keep your head and eyes down and facing the point of impact until the follow-through is completed. You will know when you hit the ball where it is going so there is no need to jerk your head and shoulders upwards to make sure. That upward jerk ruins the swing and usually results in the ball sailing over the baseline at the other end of the court. The racket should be travelling almost parallel with the ground and with its head at a slightly upward angle to your wrist.

The zip area of a sliced forehand drive. Note the high start of the swing and the way the racket strings slice under the ball in applying the spin which makes the ball skid (picture 3).

The topspin forehand made on the run. Note in picture 4 how the wrist is used to brush the racket upwards and over the ball.

A running forehand drive. Note how the smooth, right-left-right of the run sustains good body balance and so permits a flowing 'no kinks' swing. Top-class tennis demands the ability to hit well when running at top speed.

The backhand drive. Note the near horizontal swing of the racket, the use of body pivot, and the forward transference of weight so that the racket head 'chases' the ball. The player's eyes and head remain down and rock steady well after impact.

The Backhand

Anyone who has thrown a hat into a chair or dealt a pack of playing cards should know that the backhand drive in tennis uses a completely natural movement.

The secret of making your backhand drive sound and powerful lies in turning your hips and shoulders first away from the approaching ball and then strongly towards it at the point of impact; in making sure your arm, wrist, and grip are firm during the zip area of the swing; and in keeping your racket strings in contact with the ball as long as possible.

Remember that the backhand is a stroke hit sideways to the net. Give yourself ample room for the swing and, if possible, begin it early to aid a slow start and subsequent strong acceleration through the zip area. Don't let your concentration flag after impact: the extended follow-through is an equally important part of the swing. Use the lower part of your thumb to support and push forward the back part of your racket handle and always hit the ball at or just after the top of its bounce.

Above all, cast out all fear and enjoy hitting backhand drives. Study the stars at any of the televised major championships: most top players are stronger on the backhand than on the forehand wing. They may hit their forehand drives a little more powerfully but they also make more mistakes.

Back in the 1930s Australia's Vivian McGrath launched a brand new stroke on the international championship scene: the double-handed backhand. Though he and some of his successors ranked amongst the world's best players, this stroke did not gain recognition as a standard and powerful weapon until Jimmy Connors and Chris Evert won the two Wimbledon singles' championship titles in the summer of 1974.

Even today well over 50 per cent of coaches all over the world consider this proved weapon unorthodox and, really, simply a substitute for the 'classic' one-handed backhand. This is because of one easily recognisable disadvantage – the stroke's limitation

Left: To strengthen your backhand grip, put your thumb across the back of the handle and squeeze it between the thumb and the lower part of your first finger. Keep the wrist and arm in line.

Below: The topspin backhand. That slant of the racket as the player hits through the ball tells you he is applying topspin. From a position of readiness, he immediately moves his racket backwards and turns sideways. These movements continue as he goes towards the ball. Note how his weight is not brought fully forward until the moment of impact in picture 5 when his right foot is completely grounded. Picture 6 shows his weight forward, his body down, and the racket face 'chasing' the ball.

The sliced backhand. Slice is often applied by dragging the racket under the ball; this reduces power. Note in this sequence how the racket swings right through the ball, imparting the spin by a slight backward tilt of the racket head (picture 5). This spins the ball without undue loss of power.

of reach and consequent vulnerability to low and slow or wide returns.

Against this, the double-handed drive offers six valuable advantages, especially to quick, supple movers like Bjorn Borg, who won Wimbledon three years in succession in 1976–78, a rare feat and, surely, irrefutable evidence that the double-handed backhand is a great point-winner. So to those six advantages.

1 Two hands can move a racket faster than one – and power is related to racket-head speed at the moment of impact.

2 Rapidity of movement is particularly important when returning fast services; it is not chance that makes double-handed players like Frew McMillan such outstanding doubles players.

3 The short, fast swing disguises direction far more effectively than the orthodox stroke.

4 It gives extra racket stability when coping with powerful hitters.

5 The stroke stays in its 'groove' more consistently than the one-

handed, orthodox backhand.

6 There is a natural tendency to hit the ball flat or with slight topspin, compared with the tendency to slice the ball when making a normal backhand.

Fundamentally, there are three types of double-handed stroke. For a right-hander, these are, firstly, a normal backhand in which the left hand primarily helps to stabilise the racket and give it extra thrust (Borg); secondly, a normal, left-handed forehand in which the right hand mainly helps to steady the racket and pull it through slightly faster at the moment of impact; and, thirdly, a stroke in which both hands are equally effective (Evert). Many players will use all three types during a match. Some will also occasionally make a deliberate, one-handed backhand drive when the return is short or very wide. Usually the hitter has his or her hands close together, but Connors, for example, frequently slides one hand further up the handle, so constantly disturbing the harmony between the two and obtaining a much greater degree of rigidity.

The double-handed backhand provides greater racket-head acceleration without loss of racket control compared with the orthodox drive. It is slightly less flexible so precise footwork and body position are essential. Note the good balance achieved by a smooth, flowing run.

Chapter Six
Rallying

Return of Service

If you are exceptionally quick, you will be able to see a ball served to you, decide its speed and direction, and 'tell' your muscles where to move your racket, arm, and legs to return that ball in about one fifth of a second. The actual swing of a full-blooded drive from start to hit will take a further four-fifths of a second, or even more. So you need a full second from the server's hit to your return of service. This presents a special problem because many players, even at club and park level, have services which speed the ball to the receiver in three-quarters of a second or even less. Clearly, then, there is no time for a normal stroke. Wait to decide where the service is coming, and the ball will go whizzing by before your swing has reached the impact point.

There are two solutions to the problem. One is to 'pick' the direction of the service before the ball is hit; the other is to use a short, jabbing stroke that you can make very quickly. Great returners of service like Jimmy Connors and Ken Rosewall combine the two, but 'picking' direction involves advanced techniques. Start improving your return of service by adopting the short, jabbing swing which is fundamentally similar to a volley. To develop power, jab firmly and step boldly forward. Use slight underspin to assist control and keep your arm and grip braced at the moment of impact. Watch the server's racket carefully at the moment of the hit to 'read' the direction of the service early.

In returning fast serves there is no time for a long swing. So use a shorter, jabbing shot while gaining power by moving forward to meet the ball.

The Volley

If groundstrokes are the bread-and-butter of tennis, then volleys – balls hit before they bounce – are the jam. Certainly they are an essential part of tournament-class play. Any fast-moving player can run down and float back a great majority of the fastest drives until, in desperation, the opponent presses too hard and errs. The way to overcome such indomitable retrievers is to move forward and hit those floating returns before the ball has bounced, in other words to volley.

The tactic is extensively used by players with powerful services. The serve-and-run-to-the-net system came into tennis before World War I when Maurice McLoughlin of the USA introduced the cannonball service . . . and made it doubly effective by following the ball up to the net to kill off the weak returns. His was a positive, aggressive, point-winning attitude. Once near the net, he concentrated all his mental and physical strength on ending the rally with his very first volley.

This should be your aim too.

Failure to make your first volley a winner leaves you in a dangerously exposed position, vulnerable as you are to a passing shot or a lob. Put those first volleys firmly into unretrievable positions and it is your opponent who will suffer the pressures. The desperate effort to avoid your reach will lead him or her increasingly into errors. That is why, in the later stages of matches, the balance of power swings from the baseliner to the volleyer.

In serving you've been learning to throw your racket at the ball; in groundstrokes the emphasis is on swinging your racket at the ball. For the volley, you should use a short backswing and punch your racket at it.

If there is time, use your feet to get yourself sideways to the ball. If there isn't, as is often the case, pivot from your hips to get that sideways position. Keep your face near your racket head so that you can minimise parallax, an apparent change in the position of an object which is due to an actual change in the position of the observer.

The forehand volley. The ball should be punched when volleying. This means the wrist must be braced, the racket head kept well up, and the back swing shortened. The racket head should punch the ball further in front of the body than when making groundstrokes, and a strong forward step should also be made in unison with the punch if possible. The eyes should watch the ball closely. This is made easier by keeping your face close to the ball.

The forehand slice volley. When the volley is above net height, it is often unnecessary to apply any controlling spin. But if the ball is played below the net, as here, control is helped by sliding the racket strings slightly under the ball. Note in comparing this sequence with the above-net-height volley how the racket is horizontal to the ground instead of almost vertical.

Above: The forehand volley seen from the side. In volleying, seek always to attack the ball as shown in this sequence. Note the short back-swing in pictures 2 and 3 and the thrusting, punching follow-through (picture 4 onwards). That forward step to meet the ball is also important, as is the powerful, right shoulder thrust.

Centre pictures: Effective volleying is an essential factor in a champion's stroke armoury. It can also make for pleasing gracefulness when you are a Vitas Gerulaitis.

Below: The backhand volley also has to be punched. Alertness is all important here. Note the bent knees and the racket up and forwards, with the left hand supporting it at its throat in readiness for the firm grip and strong punch shown in pictures 4 and 5. Note, too, the head of the racket above the wrist, the power-building forward step while punching the ball, and the shortened follow-through of the stroke.

Right: Low volleys. Strive in all shots to hold your racket firmly and keep both eyes as near to the racket face as possible. In the case of low volleys, move forward to the ball, meeting it just in front of the leading leg, bend your knees so that your hand does not drop below racket level, brace your wrist, tilt the racket (slightly upwards for the forehand, backwards for the backhand), and drag the strings gently under the ball to give controlling backspin.

Opposite, top: The sliced backhand volley. Slice is also generally needed to hold the ball on the racket strings and thus control it when making a backhand volley below net height. Note the angle of the racket in the back swing, the deeply bent knees, and the careful watching of the ball. In pictures 2 and 3 see how the racket strings are tilted slightly backwards just before meeting the ball and how that tilt increases as the racket slides under the ball to impart the spin.

Opposite, centre left: The forehand half volley. You will be caught sometimes by returns which force you to hit the ball as it bounces (in what is called a half volley). Here the player makes a forehand half volley. Watching the ball intently throughout the entire stroke, he moves towards it and starts bending his knees. Still moving to the ball in picture 2, he tilts his racket slightly forwards. Then, swinging the racket firmly but gently to meet the ball as it bounces, his racket tilt slightly less pronounced, his body rotates with the swing.

Opposite, centre right: The backhand half volley. As with the forehand half volley, get both eyes as near to the racket face as possible by bending your knees and leaning towards the ball.

Left: The drop volley. It is sometimes possible to win a point with a volley which gently drops the ball over the net, leaving your opponent stranded on the baseline. A risky but pleasing shot to make, it is easy to become addicted . . . and disastrous.

The powerful forward run and the strong look of the racket swing suggest a deep volley to come. Then there is a slight slowing down while the racket curls itself gently but firmly under the ball in dropping it just over the net. Note how carefully the player watches the ball on and off the racket and the deep knee bend. See how he uses his wrist to impart the backspin which stops the ball bounding forward after bouncing and also helps to lessen that bounce.

The overhead smash. This sequence demonstrates the rules of sound overhead play. First, turn sideways, meantime carefully watching the ball. Second, get your racket into position for the kill right away. Note that the player moves his racket straight upwards and not with the long back-swing used in serving. Third, use your left (free) hand as a sighter by pointing at the ball. Fourth, move into position with firm but short skipping steps. Fifth, throw every scrap of power into the smash. Note how he pivots all his energy into the stroke, his shoulders turning square to the net at impact before sweeping his racket strongly past his left leg and returning to his ready position.

The Overhead Smash

Nothing brings a crowd to its feet quicker or earns louder, more vigorous clapping than a ferociously smashed lob. One player rushes to the net, the other hoists the ball skywards, and all eyes watch its upward path. The net-rusher pauses, back pedals, waits and then, as the ball drops within reach, crunches it down into the opponent's court, maybe to bounce irretrievably over the back or side netting.

Successful overhead smashes demand one quality above all others: utter determination to end the rally once and for all. There can be no room for doubt and anxiety, especially if the lob is high. The ball will be dropping almost vertically and fast so it has to be hit approximately at right angles to its descending path. To make contact with the square inch (6.45 cm^2) or so in the centre of the racket strings, the racket head must travel very fast: any tentative, half-hearted swing is almost certain to produce a mis-hit. Even more than in volleying, there is no time for hesitation. The ball must be watched, the player positioned, and the racket head thrown vigorously at the ball when it comes into reach, the player perhaps jumping high to meet it. As the ball is clobbered, the thought should be 'my point'.

Scorn all safety-first thoughts of letting the ball bounce before you hit it. Previous shots in the rally have created the chance of winning the point. Seize it confidently: confidence breeds increased confidence.

Roscoe Tanner's 128 mph (206 km) services are now world famous but little is written about his overhead smashes when lobbed at the net. His pointing hand, racket at the ready with time to spare, and those eyes fixed steadfastly on the descending ball tell clearly that his smash is every scrap the equal of his service.

The Lob

Back in 1878 P. F. Hadow wrecked S. W. Gore's bid to retain the Wimbledon men's singles title by hoisting the ball over Gore's reach and near to the baseline each time he ran forward to volley. Thus the lob was born. Yet, in spite of Hadow's exemplary use of it, this valuable attacking shot has remained the least exploited one in tennis. Nine times out of ten it is used only when a player is in such dire difficulties that he or she has virtually no choice but to lob. This situation is always crystal clear to the opposing player, who naturally anticipates it and moves backward to kill the ball with a powerful smash.

The ideal time to lob is when your opponent is moving, preferably forwards in expectation of a fast passing shot. Make your lob by ignoring the opponent completely and concentrating on the baseline at the far end of the court. Hit the ball with a firm, long follow-through so that it crosses the net in an arc which reaches a high point of approximately 18 feet (5·49 m) above ground level right over the net. Hit precisely in this way from your baseline, a ball without spin on a windless day must obey the laws of physics and come down exactly on the baseline at the other end of the court.

Imagine a hoop high over the net and aim the ball through it. Depending on whether you hit the ball inside or outside your baseline, that imaginary hoop will have to be moved slightly backwards or forwards. The basic fact to remember is that a ball hit without spin will travel in a parabola with the downward path of the ball mirroring its upward flight. So forget the opponent, think only of where you are relative to the net, and concentrate on the opposite baseline, making that your target. Diagram 8 illustrates the effects of back and top spin on a lob of similar strength, and Diagram 9 shows the technique for playing the stroke.

The Drop Shot

The drop shot has an important part to play when you want to vary the length of your replies. This is the shot which drops the ball just over the net so that it dies quickly and has the opponent scrambling forwards to lift the ball back across the net. In making a drop shot, two factors are important: firstly, the ball must not bounce high after crossing the net, and secondly it should surprise your opponent.

To prevent the ball bouncing too high, hit it at the top of its bounce and with slight underspin. There can be no 'nevers' in tennis but, almost invariably, if your aim is to hit the ball at the top of its bounce and yet not give your opponent liberal time to run forward and make an aggressive

Diagram 8: Assuming there is no wind, a ball hit at *h* without spin (or flat) but with sufficient strength to reach the highest point of its flight exactly over the net will land on the baseline (point *b*) as in flight-line 1. Hit with the same strength but with backspin, the ball will descend more like line 2. Hit with some topspin and the same strength, the second part of the lob dips quite sharply, the ball bounding away rapidly after bouncing as in line 3.

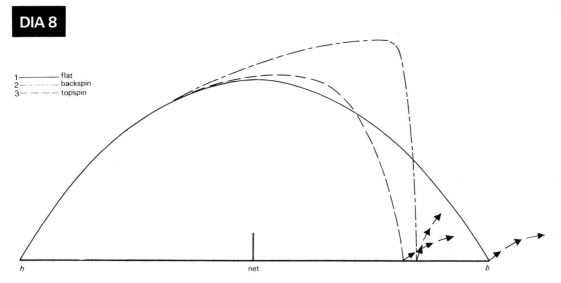

DIA 8

1 ——————— flat
2 — · — · — · — backspin
3 — — — — topspin

h　　　　　　　　net　　　　　　　　*b*

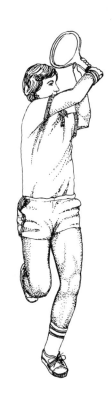

Diagram 9: Few players feel happy trying to subdue fast-moving opponents who chase down everything and send back successions of 'moonball' drives that clear the net by 15 feet (4·6 m) or so before landing deep in court. The diagram shows how to brush the ball with the racket strings to impart topspin. This makes the ball dip sharply in flight, so minimising the risk of hitting over the baseline.

Left: Always make your drop shot when the ball is at or above net height.

reply, you should avoid making a drop shot when you are less than 6 feet (1·83 m) in front of your own baseline.

Try to avoid lofting the ball too. Hit it positively and with a definite backspin which makes it bite into the court and then skid or stop. Since the shortest distance between two points is a straight line, normally hit your drop shots straight rather than across the court, to hurry your opponent.

49

Chapter Seven
Tactics

A Game of Action

Ignoring until later the mental demands the game imposes, tennis can be described as a sport which tests physical qualities to the utmost limits.

Fitness is sometimes related to the six S's: speed, suppleness, skill, strength, stamina, and soul. All are essential, but to the inexperienced onlooker speed and suppleness probably seem the most obvious requirements. It is easy to see why. Take service for a start. Most male players of professional tournament standard serve at a speed which sends the ball from their rackets to the opposite baseline – the usual receiving position – in approximately 800 milliseconds (from now on abbreviated to mscs).

Reaction time is the name we give to the time it takes to see an event taking place, to decide what response to make, and to take the initial action to fulfil that response. The British School of Motoring and *Tennis*, the magazine I edited for many years, both carried out exhaustive measurements on the reaction times of hundreds of thousands of subjects in their respective fields. Their findings concur and Table 2 sets out their joint statistics.

	Category of player	Reaction time
1	ultra-fast	200 mscs
2	fast	400 mscs
3	average	700 mscs

Table 2

Athleticism, effort, mobility. and determination: these are just some of the qualities which shine out when great champions are in pursuit of major titles. Tom Okker, Buster Mottram, Jimmy Connors, and Evonne Cawley, all contenders in the 1978 Wimbledon singles championships.

Great tennis stars like Connors and Bjorn Borg are in category 1, many fast, top-line players fall somewhere along the continuum of category 1 to 2, and the majority of ordinary to good players could be placed somewhere between category 2 and 3.

Normal tennis strokes take anything from 300 to 1 000 mscs from inception to the moment of hitting the ball. So Borg at his best is able to react and complete a responding hit in $200 + 300 = 500$ mscs, the exact time it takes for a Roscoe Tanner cannonball service to reach him. Lesser players are nowhere near so fast. The ball has passed them before they make a stroke, in many cases before they move. A similar or even faster situation exists when one player is at the net and the other is on the baseline. Both have to move faster than is theoretically possible. This can only be achieved by reading the game. In other words, anticipation becomes a vital part of play.

This necessity to move quicker than is seemingly possible is what makes tennis the perfect, all-action game for those who master the basics and progress beyond that stage.

Diagram 10: The three zones in your court. When hitting in the red zone, reduce risk-taking. In the green zone, attack. In the yellow zone, discriminate, depending on your confidence and your opponent's quality. The arc *ab* indicates the alert zone to which you should try to return after making each stroke. This is normally the position on court which bisects all the angles and depths open to your opponent.

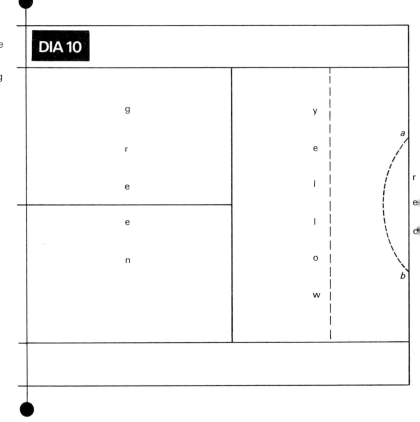

— — — interim extension
to green zone

a b 'alert' zone

Zoning

Just as Albert Einstein first mastered his multiplication tables before becoming probably the most imaginative mathematical physicist in history, so would-be crack tennis players should completely absorb basic tactical techniques before advancing too deeply into the subtleties one sees in thinker-players like Manuel Orantes and Arthur Ashe.

An understanding of zoning is an invaluable tool in tactical development. Begin by taking a look at Diagram 10. This shows one half of a court divided into three zones – green, yellow, and red – somewhat in the manner of traffic signals, and with similar implications.

The red zone lies behind the baseline. Unless your opponent is up at the net, you've very little chance in this position of hitting a ball with such pace and placement that it is unreachable. He or she will be 26 yards (23·77 m) or more away from you and a fast drive will take at least 1½ seconds to reach the far baseline. In that time your opponent can prob-

ably run 12 or more yards (10·97 m), the total width of the doubles court. So why waste your energy? It is normally better to hit for depth – say within 4 feet (1·22 m) of the baseline – and towards a corner, while hoping for a shorter reply next time. Red, then, means hold your position: wait and see.

Green, on the other hand, means go. If you can make your shot in that area between the net and the service line, you must play aggressively. With the ball at or above net height, you should be able to drive or volley beyond your opponent's reach. If the ball is low, it may well be preferable to stroke it deep into a corner and then move into the net, determined to make a winning volley off the next return.

The yellow zone between service and baseline is essentially a stop/go region. Sometimes you will be able to attack, and sometimes you will be forced to temporise. The diagram shows a dotted line bisecting this zone. As your prowess grows, you will be able to extend the green zone back from the service line towards that imaginary line and beyond it. This will happen all the faster as growing confidence allows you to hit the ball as it rises after bouncing. Mastery of this technique will inevitably increase your ability to apply pressure to your opponent when it comes to varying your shot length.

Always expect the shot you hit to be good. Avoid the natural inclination to watch anxiously the ball you have just hit. Instead move immediately to the position on court that bisects the angles and depths open to your opponent when making the reply. This normally lies somewhere along the arc shown in Diagram 10. Note, incidentally, how it curves slightly in front of the baseline. Reaching that area after every stroke you make will involve continuous movement. This constant movement neutralises body inertia so, even if your op-

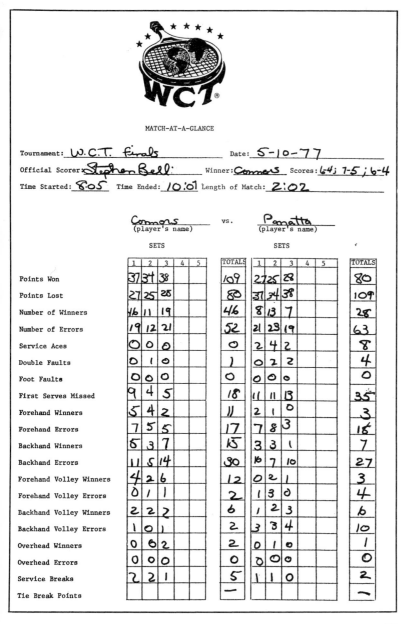

Table 3: This breakdown of the 1977 World Championship of Tennis final play-off between Jimmy Connors and Adriano Panatta demonstrates the truth of the statement that it is mistakes that lose matches.

MATCH-AT-A-GLANCE

Tournament: W.C.T. finals   Date: 5-10-77
Official Scorer: Stephen Bell   Winner: Connors   Scores: 6-4; 7-5; 6-4
Time Started: 8.05   Time Ended: 10.01   Length of Match: 2:02

Connors (player's name) vs. Panatta (player's name)

	Connors SETS 1	2	3	4	5	TOTALS	Panatta SETS 1	2	3	4	5	TOTALS
Points Won	37	34	38			109	27	25	28			80
Points Lost	27	25	28			80	37	34	38			109
Number of Winners	16	11	19			46	8	13	7			28
Number of Errors	19	12	21			52	21	23	19			63
Service Aces	0	0	0			0	2	4	2			8
Double Faults	0	1	0			1	0	2	2			4
Foot Faults	0	0	0			0	0	0	0			0
First Serves Missed	9	4	5			18	11	11	13			35
Forehand Winners	5	4	2			11	2	1	0			3
Forehand Errors	7	5	5			17	7	8	3			18
Backhand Winners	5	3	7			15	3	3	1			7
Backhand Errors	11	5	14			30	10	7	10			27
Forehand Volley Winners	4	2	6			12	0	2	1			3
Forehand Volley Errors	0	1	1			2	1	3	0			4
Backhand Volley Winners	2	2	2			6	1	2	3			6
Backhand Volley Errors	1	0	1			2	3	3	4			10
Overhead Winners	0	0	2			2	0	1	0			1
Overhead Errors	0	0	0			0	0	0	0			0
Service Breaks	2	2	1			5	1	1	0			2
Tie Break Points						—						—

ponent's return is unexpectedly deep, you will be able to retreat more easily than if both your feet were planted firmly on the ground.

Playing on Weaknesses

Developing sound and effective strokes is, unquestionably, important. But learning how best to deploy them is even more important. All too often in tournaments and matches one sees a beautifully fluent stroke-maker brought down by a seemingly ungainly opponent who is able not merely to return all those flowing shots but also to place the replies in areas of the court where they wreak the greatest amount of havoc.

In this context, it is imperative to understand that even at the topmost levels of the game matches are won and lost not primarily by the spectacular shots of one or other player but by the mistakes they make. Table 3 on page 53 shows a breakdown of the match between Jimmy Connors and Adriano Panatta in the 1977 World Championship of Tennis final play-off. Both men are notably aggressive yet the analysis proves that Panatta's greater crop of mistakes decided the outcome.

Mistakes usually flow more readily from a player's weakness, and the first task in any match should be to discover just what the weakness or weaknesses are. Then one can decide on an overall strategy and the point-by-point tactics to make it effective.

To give a simple example, your opponent may be a man with a slow but steady sliced backhand and a powerful but erratic forehand. The obvious plan would seem to be an all-out attack on his backhand but it is probable that he has experienced such attacks before . . . and learned to cope with them. It might therefore prove more profitable to attack his forehand with wide returns in order to open up that slower backhand. For the first couple of points you could test his strong forehand and then follow up with a straight attack on the backhand for the next couple. On game points either way it would again probably be best to go first for the strength, on the theory that he may move away to the backhand to give himself more chance of running round the ball to use his fearsome forehand whenever he gets a shot to that weak side. At a time when world rankings showed Britain's Sue Barker in the first six and Israel's Paulina Peled way down in the hundreds, Paulina won twice, once very easily, by using those very tactics to make the general strategy of attack-the-strength work.

The Importance of Surprise

Surprise is the essence of effective tactics. Repeat the same shots and sequences over and over again and even players reputedly far below your own standard will probably overcome them. Variety is important.

Diagram 11: Eight sequences which can put your opponent under pressure.
Sequence 1 First shot to *h* or *l*. Follow with an approach shot to *m* and go to the net.
Sequence 2 First shot to *e* or *i*, second to *p* and run to the net.
Sequence 3 First shot to *e* or *i*, second a drop shot to *a*.
Sequence 4 First shot to *m*, second to *p*, third to *m*, fourth a wrong-footer back to *m*.
Sequence 5 First shot to *e* or *i*, second shot deep to *m* and run in.
Sequence 6 First shot to *h*, second deep to *o* and run in to the net.
Sequence 7 First shot to *e*, second deep to *n* and run in.
Sequence 8 First shot to *h*, second to *m*, third to *d*.

DIA 11

And remember: it can be applied in many ways. Differences of pace and spin are useful but changes of length are often more effective. Then again, most players become adept at running backwards and forwards along the baseline. Force them to turn and run back to the side they have just left – occasionally, of course – and you may well disrupt their rhythm.

Hit the ball short to one sideline and then deep to the opposite corner and you will make things even more difficult. Not only will you be running them in unaccustomed directions, but when running diagonally backwards they will be unable to watch the ball closely and also keep an eye open to check where you are moving. You can therefore surprise them by moving forwards to volley their returns when they think you are staying on the baseline, and vice versa.

Learn to string your shots together in pre-determined, intensely practised sequences. If the first shot of any sequence is not returned as expected, simply play a temporising shot and wait for another suitable return to start the sequence once more.

To take just a single example, in competitive tennis something like one in every three shots hit by your opponent will direct the ball into the circle marked 'T' (for typical) in Diagram 11 (excluding, of course, services and pre-supposing that you are right handed). This affords you valuable opportunities for starting sequences of placements which put your opponent under pressure and win you many points. Looking at Diagram 11, imagine you are on the baseline and the ball falls at a comfortable height and speed in 'T'. There are eight sequences for you to practise. Later, you can begin to work out some sequences of your own aimed to make your opponent twist, turn, and run as uncomfortably as possible.

Learning set sequences will not make you into an unthinking robot. On the contrary, if you have up your sleeve half a dozen sequences you can produce almost as though blindfolded, your mind will be freer to study the play in a detached manner and so extemporise other series of shots to break your opponent down and win points and games.

Occasionally you may be able to beat an opponent simply by chasing down and returning every ball until he or she makes mistakes from sheer frustration. More often, such purely defensive methods are less profitable than those in which you scheme while you run. You may discover that your opponent is uneasy when you vary the pace or length of your returns. So you hit your first return high and soft, your second lower and slightly faster, the next a shade slower but shorter and with backspin, and so on.

Watch each ball carefully as it comes towards you. Decide quickly how difficult it will be to handle. Maybe it will take all your skill merely to return it. Perhaps it is not going to be full length so you will be able to play an angled, fairly fast, court-opening shot. But it may be that your previous return has forced a weak, short reply. If you are really alert, you should spot this the moment the ball leaves your opponent's racket and you can be moving well forward for your kill half a second or more before the ball crosses the net.

Learn to peak your concentration during that fiftieth part of a second spanning the before and after of each stroke made by your opponent and then discipline yourself to treat each ball strictly on its merits. The best houses are constructed brick by brick. The best wins are achieved by playing ball after ball to the best of your ability without any anxiety about winning the next game.

Concentration involves focussing your whole mind on the match in progress. Help this by keeping your eyes strictly within the confines of the court; looking at your feet between points is one little wrinkle. When your mind is invaded by stray thoughts, never pursue them. Instead, switch to something positive, like determining to lengthen the follow-through of your strokes or looking for an extra weakness in your opponent. Concentrate all your mental and physical efforts on doing the best you can with each ball that comes your way and you will find yourself winning points, games, sets, and matches.

Chapter Eight
The Psychology of Winning

Winning at tennis begins with the recognition that we live in a highly competitive society, that for every winner there must be many losers. At Wimbledon, for instance, there are 128 acceptances for the men's singles, of whom 127 must finish anywhere from second to 128th.

In order to win, therefore, you must, if you are a truly ambitious player, commit yourself utterly and completely to victory. You must acknowledge that in the process you will lose many more times than you win before you reach the world's top sixty or so. Yet you must never accept defeat lightly. Be prepared, nay eager, to throw every scrap of energy and guile into competition, knowing yet disdaining the fact that on many occasions you may be made to look a fool. Self-belief, fed on sheer love of the game and competition, must override all the doubts which arise from defeat. See those defeats as the rungs of a ladder leading upwards to the pinnacles of skill. Recognise that those pinnacles are probably higher than you can even conceive. Then banish them from your mind while striving shot by shot to become ever a shade better than you were yesterday.

Perhaps surprisingly, few people are willing to take this chance. Most of them 'cop out'. They delude themselves, claiming that they only play for exercise, companionship, or as an escape from the arduous nature of everyday life. Future champions can often be spotted even before they reach their teens. They are usually so totally absorbed in the game that side issues of success or failure never enter their minds. All they want to do is get on a court to strive and think and play and keep on advancing. (Table 4 shows an interesting analysis of various aspects of the personality of the average champion.)

The first requirement, then, for becoming a winner is total abandonment of all role-playing, false pride, and wishful thinking. Never ask 'can I become a good player?' Instead, patiently, thoughtfully, and with unremitting tenacity determine to become one. Fill your mind with the determination that the very next shot you play will leave you a slightly better player than you were before you made it. Give even more concentration to that shot than you would if stimulated by a competitive situation. As each ball comes towards you, concentrate simply on dealing with it as best you can, whether it be an offensive, temporising, or defensive shot.

All this implies a constant striving to improve technique. Competitive success – winning – derives from

The video tape-recorder can play a useful part in the recognition of tactical weaknesses. Here British professional coach Malcolm Gibb helps a top-ranking junior eliminate errors of tactics and technique.

16 P.F. TEST PROFILE

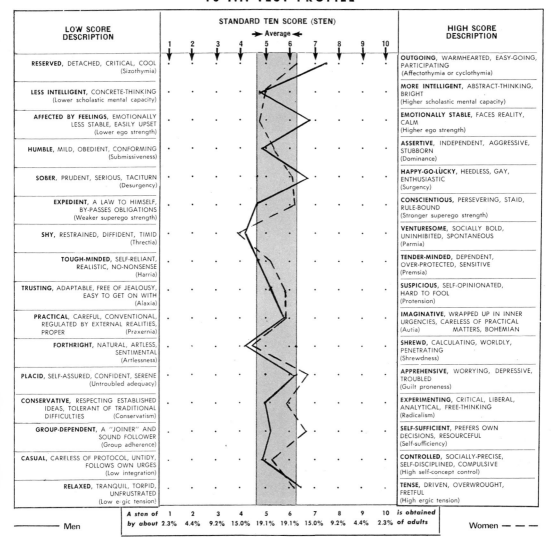

LOW SCORE DESCRIPTION	STANDARD TEN SCORE (STEN) →Average←	HIGH SCORE DESCRIPTION
RESERVED, DETACHED, CRITICAL, COOL (Sizothymia)		OUTGOING, WARMHEARTED, EASY-GOING, PARTICIPATING (Affectothymia or cyclothymia)
LESS INTELLIGENT, CONCRETE-THINKING (Lower scholastic mental capacity)		MORE INTELLIGENT, ABSTRACT-THINKING, BRIGHT (Higher scholastic mental capacity)
AFFECTED BY FEELINGS, EMOTIONALLY LESS STABLE, EASILY UPSET (Lower ego strength)		EMOTIONALLY STABLE, FACES REALITY, CALM (Higher ego strength)
HUMBLE, MILD, OBEDIENT, CONFORMING (Submissiveness)		ASSERTIVE, INDEPENDENT, AGGRESSIVE, STUBBORN (Dominance)
SOBER, PRUDENT, SERIOUS, TACITURN (Desurgency)		HAPPY-GO-LUCKY, HEEDLESS, GAY, ENTHUSIASTIC (Surgency)
EXPEDIENT, A LAW TO HIMSELF, BY-PASSES OBLIGATIONS (Weaker superego strength)		CONSCIENTIOUS, PERSEVERING, STAID, RULE-BOUND (Stronger superego strength)
SHY, RESTRAINED, DIFFIDENT, TIMID (Threctia)		VENTURESOME, SOCIALLY BOLD, UNINHIBITED, SPONTANEOUS (Parmia)
TOUGH-MINDED, SELF-RELIANT, REALISTIC, NO-NONSENSE (Harria)		TENDER-MINDED, DEPENDENT, OVER-PROTECTED, SENSITIVE (Premsia)
TRUSTING, ADAPTABLE, FREE OF JEALOUSY, EASY TO GET ON WITH (Alaxia)		SUSPICIOUS, SELF-OPINIONATED, HARD TO FOOL (Protension)
PRACTICAL, CAREFUL, CONVENTIONAL, REGULATED BY EXTERNAL REALITIES, PROPER (Praxernia)		IMAGINATIVE, WRAPPED UP IN INNER URGENCIES, CARELESS OF PRACTICAL MATTERS, BOHEMIAN (Autia)
FORTHRIGHT, NATURAL, ARTLESS, SENTIMENTAL (Artlessness)		SHREWD, CALCULATING, WORLDLY, PENETRATING (Shrewdness)
PLACID, SELF-ASSURED, CONFIDENT, SERENE (Untroubled adequacy)		APPREHENSIVE, WORRYING, DEPRESSIVE, TROUBLED (Guilt proneness)
CONSERVATIVE, RESPECTING ESTABLISHED IDEAS, TOLERANT OF TRADITIONAL DIFFICULTIES (Conservatism)		EXPERIMENTING, CRITICAL, LIBERAL, ANALYTICAL, FREE-THINKING (Radicalism)
GROUP-DEPENDENT, A "JOINER" AND SOUND FOLLOWER (Group adherence)		SELF-SUFFICIENT, PREFERS OWN DECISIONS, RESOURCEFUL (Self-sufficiency)
CASUAL, CARELESS OF PROTOCOL, UNTIDY, FOLLOWS OWN URGES (Low integration)		CONTROLLED, SOCIALLY-PRECISE, SELF-DISCIPLINED, COMPULSIVE (High self-concept control)
RELAXED, TRANQUIL, TORPID, UNFRUSTRATED (Low ergic tension)		TENSE, DRIVEN, OVERWROUGHT, FRETFUL (High ergic tension)

A sten of	1	2	3	4	5	6	7	8	9	10	is obtained
by about	2.3%	4.4%	9.2%	15.0%	19.1%	19.1%	15.0%	9.2%	4.4%	2.3%	of adults

———— Men   Women — — —

confidence, and true confidence springs from all-round competence, the elimination of weaknesses of technique, tactics, and temperament.

Tactical knowledge comes from constant, thoughtful, imaginative play and the study of other people's systems and methods. Temperamental development demands continuous monitoring of one's own attitudes and behaviour. It includes total dedication and total rejection of all forms of competitive evasion. No one can know in advance whether he or she will achieve greatness. So you must banish doubts about the future and strive to achieve your full potential,

never being satisfied with less than the best performance of which you are capable.

If this is the target, it becomes easier to de-personalise the stars and near contenders who are constantly crossing one's competitive path. One can ignore the name across the net and, instead, see only a tennis racket being moved around the court by a pair of legs and swung by an arm attached to a headless body. One can play the ball instead of the player, countering each return with the best shot available instead of trying an impossibility because the opponent is Jimmy Connors.

Table 4: The Sixteen Personality Factors System devised by Professor Raymond Cattell divides personality into sixteen main categories. The graph shows where twelve male and twenty female world champions lie along each continuum. Note that world champions vary from average people in being restrained, yet forthright. Men also tend to be outgoing, emotionally stable, surgent (full of go), but somewhat tense. Women tend towards guilt complexes but are more self sufficient than men. These are averages, remember.

Chapter Nine
Practice and Match Preparation

Electronics harnessed for the intensive methods of modern coaching: the measurement of coach Peter Williams' service during a British Professional Tennis Coaches Association advanced course on world-class serving directed by the author.

Practice makes perfect, they say. What they never add is that practice, if it is to be effective, demands even greater concentration and effort than match play.

The reason is simple. Each time you make a movement you produce a series of electrical currents which flow through your nerves. Keep on repeating the same movement and you burn into your neural network a path which tends to standardise further repetition. An over-simplified analogy is the track made by a car's

wheels going up and down a narrow driveway day after day; after a while it is difficult to turn the wheels out of the track. Similarly, as almost every close match reveals, the constantly practised tennis stroke becomes habitual. Comes the crisis, the player reverts to that basic type determined by inherited character and environmental conditioning (i.e. practice).

Because the vast majority of tennis strokes are slightly unnatural, the need for intense concentration when practising is overwhelming. Anything less will, almost surely, lead to the development of faulty movements and the deeper these 'burn' themselves into your neural make-up, the more difficult it is to replace them with correct 'patterns'.

The length of time anyone can concentrate on a single factor is strictly limited. Depending on basic personality, it varies from around 4 to 10 minutes. After that the brain is likely to slip into a waking sleep and resulting movements degenerate into dangerous habits. So, when learning any new stroke or tactic, or when trying to iron out kinks which have developed, work in small bursts. After, say, 8 minutes, switch to something else, maybe your service instead of your forehand drive. Carry out your learning or rectifying practice under 'no pressure' conditions. Have your partner feed you comparatively easy balls. Only when you feel smoothly 'grooved' should you begin to rehearse under increasing pressure until you can handle simulated match-play conditions.

The development of sound, stable strokes can be significantly assisted by daily spells of mental rehearsal. A handful of top liners already use this technique. If you vividly *think* a movement, you can generate nerve currents which are identical to those set up when actually making those movements.

You have studied this book and, maybe, had professional coaching, perhaps with electronic aids. All very helpful but in the end it is you and you alone who can make it work. Only if you live tennis and play wherever and whenever you can, like Michael Leach under the railway arches, do you stand any chance of becoming a great player.

Theoretically there should be no need ever to go on court to practise, but thoroughly authenticated research shows that the best progress is achieved through a mixture of actual practice and mental rehearsal. So, to be specific, 2 hours spent on court practice three or four times a week supplemented by 15 minutes mental rehearsal every morning and evening should result in quite pleasing advancement for any ambitious amateur wishing to reach county-team levels who possesses the right enthusiasm, mental discipline, and power of applied concentration.

Mental fitness and playing prowess are normally increased by improved physical fitness. In tennis terms, fitness consists of stamina, speed, suppleness, skill, strength and soul, not specially in that order. Of these, stamina is the easiest to increase. The way is through running, miles and miles of running with the object of driving further and further back the onset of searing lungs and aching muscles. And no matter how long that takes, you must find the will to battle through the 'pain barrier'. A firm word of warning: unless you already exercise fairly extensively, consult your doctor before embarking on any campaign of vigorous physical training. Given the go-ahead, start moderately and take three or four weeks to establish your current peak capacity. Then strive to increase it. Stamina is also increased by smooth, flowing, efficient movements. A flowing player like, say, Ilie Nastase imposes smaller demands on whole heaps of muscles than the contortionists to be seen in almost any club or public park.

Loss of blood sugar in the brain decreases the concentration so take carbohydrate-packed meals before playing and allow at least 3 hours between eating and playing. On court, supplement your energy with a revitalising liquid: Dynamo and Accolade are widely used.

Nervousness is a function of adrenal gland activity. If you are not nervous before an important match, you are not keyed up for total action. So welcome your nervousness and harness it to peak performance by fixing your mind on specific activities, such as hitting each ball just after the top of its bounce and treating every ball that comes to you strictly on its merits.

Above all, learn to enjoy the challenge of good play and competition. Respect your opponent's good shots and say to yourself each time he or she hits one, 'Now I'll show you a better one.' That way you will gain fuller enjoyment and make the quickest improvement.

Chapter Ten

Where Do You Take It From Here?

A group of Americans visiting Africa once taught the Kopji tribe to play basketball. Tall, strong and lithe, the Kopjis quickly showed superb form. So much so that the visitors suggested a match with a top American professional league team. But the Kopjis did not want to know . . . because it would have involved scoring. And that, they declared, would spoil the game.

Their austere attitude to games is shared by only a handful of tennis players. The rest, be they English, Russian, Australian, American, Italian, French, you name it, have the inborn need to compare themselves with their peers, whether they be the same nationality or not.

Fortunately most tennis-playing nations are controlled by people who recognise this need, people who themselves organise or encourage others to devise and stage tournaments, matches, and other competitions covering all age groups from pre-teens right through to the over 65s and, in some cases, the over 70s, 75s, and even 80s. Normally, the competitive ladder starts with the teenies, the under 12s to be precise. As the child grows up, he or she progresses through the under 14, 16, 18, and 21 age groups. Thereafter it tends to become a free-for-all, though in the USA they resume age gradings with the 35s and over. Players are not confined to a specific age group. Juniors can play in sections for older people up to the 35s. At this point one has to be over the prescribed age.

The more important events are recognised by the appropriate national or regional body and publicised in their official listings of tournaments. Other competitions (like the various closed county championships, parks tournaments, and others promoted by newspapers, hospitals or other organisations) have various restrictions that remove any need for official sanction, though most such events enjoy the blessing of the relevant governing association.

Club championships flourish everywhere in the world and these usually form the starting point for a player's competitive career. Your local professional coach or sports store should, if any use, be fully acquainted with the competitive scene in the area. If not, then the relevant national tennis association will be able to help. The addresses of national associations can be obtained on request – self-addressed, stamped envelopes, please – from the International Tennis Federation, Barons Court, London W14 9EG, England. If you live in Britain, your queries should be directed to The Lawn Tennis Association, Barons Court, London, W14 9EG. USA queries should go to the United States Tennis Association Inc., 51 East 42nd Street, New York, NY 10017. In Britain and the USA the various regional tennis associations can also advise you. Secretaries' addresses are printed in the national tennis association handbook. Affiliated clubs are sent a copy and a call to your local club's secretary will probably yield most of the information you seek.

Never fear entering a tournament. If it is too strong for your standard, your entry will not be accepted. And you can try something weaker. You may lose but you will learn much and gain more pleasure from the next few you enter and with application you will soon graduate into the experienced competitor category.

Once you have digested this book you should take professional coaching . . . and from a member of your national professional tennis coaches' association.

Above all, treat tennis as a source of pleasure. If that is the only lesson you learn from this book, I shall have served you well.

Index

Acknowledgments

People The author and publishers gratefully acknowledge the assistance of Chris Bradnam, who we believe will be a member of Britain's Davis Cup team before this book is one year old, Stella Risner, whose tennis court we used, and Neil Collings of Chandlersford, Hampshire, who posed for some of the grip photographs.

Illustrations Details of photographic credits are as follows. Allsport, Morden – Tony Duffy: jacket and cover, title page, 9 top right, 47 top, 50, 51 right; Allsport – Don Morley: 42 centre; Allsport – Steve Powell: 19, 51 left; Frank Baron, Sporting Pictures (UK), London: front endpapers, 43; Diana Burnett, Bromley: 18 left, back endpaper; Derek Davis, Keston: 8 top left; Dunlop Sports Co. Ltd, London: 14, 17, 18 right; Albert Evans, Balham: 56; General Foods (UK) Ltd: 26 left; Hamlyn Group Picture Library – Diana Burnett: 9 left, 11, 12 bottom, 13, 20, 21 top, 22, 28, 33 top, 36 top, 37 top, 44 centre and bottom; Hamlyn Group Picture Library – Don Morley/Allsport: 15, 31, 32–33 bottom, 34, 35, 36–37 bottom, 38–39, 40, 41, 42 top and bottom, 44 top, 45, 46–47 bottom, 49 bottom; C. M. Jones, London: 8 bottom left, 8 right, 21 bottom, 26 right, 30, 58, 59; Le-Roye Productions, Beckenham: 9 bottom right; H. W. Neale, Sutton: 12 top, 24–25. Diagrams 1–8, 10 and 11 are the work of the Hayward Art Group, while the charts used in Tables 3 and 4 are copyright of World Championship Tennis Inc. and Professor Raymond Cattell of the Minnesota Institute of Personality Measurement respectively.